KU-114-122

NORTH ITALIAN DRAWINGS
OF THE QUATTROCENTO

DRAWINGS OF THE GREAT MASTERS

A SERIES OF VOLUMES UNDER THE GENERAL EDITOR-
SHIP OF A. E. POPHAM AND K. T. PARKER

NORTH ITALIAN DRAWINGS
of the
QUATTROCENTO

BY

K. T. PARKER

With

Seventy-two Illustrations
in Collotype

1927

LONDON

ERNEST BENN LIMITED

BOUVERIE HOUSE, FLEET STREET

DEDICATED TO

HENRY OPPENHEIMER

Made and Printed in Great Britain at
The Mayflower Press, Plymouth. William Brendon & Son, Ltd.

NORTH ITALIAN DRAWINGS
OF THE QUATTROCENTO

THE scope of the present volume, in regard to both time and place, is clearly prescribed, and little comment need therefore be made on it. Comprised, as it is, of the provinces of Lombardy, Emilia and the Veneto, Northern Italy forms a unit so distinct and generally recognised in art-history, that in separating its schools of painting from those of Tuscany and Umbria, we shall adopt a quite usual method of classification. Apart from precedent, a glance at the map is enough to suggest it, and a survey of history provides ample corroboration of its justness, if such indeed be required. Moreover, that Upper and Central Italy differed appreciably in artistic temperament even during the fifteenth century, is a fact that has often been noticed, though by its very nature that difference is hard to define. It becomes clear enough at a later date, when Venetian colourism breaks away from the *disegno* of the Florentine and Roman Schools entirely, and when, indeed, the followers of a Titian are almost at open feud with the partisans of a Michael Angelo. For the period which concerns us here, the underlying cause of disparity is, however, essentially the same : art in the North of Italy partakes a less constructive character than it does notably in Tuscany, and sentiment tends to become a factor more divorced from the element of form.

It stands to reason that when dealing with the North Italian Schools as a separate chapter of Renaissance art, it is yet essential to keep the great Tuscan and Umbrian masters in view, since their orbit of influence extended far beyond their native provinces, and they contributed in no small measure to the development of their North Italian contemporaries. The reader need hardly be told what a profound impress was left by Donatello at Padua, or at a later date, by Leonardo da Vinci at Milan ; and he will readily understand that while it is necessary to impose certain definite lines of separation to our subject, our outlook should yet embrace the whole field of Italian art. In point

5

of time, too, we shall need to take considerable latitude from hard-and-fast classification, though doubtless the opposition in a more or less literal sense of the terms *Quattrocento* and *Cinquecento* is largely justified. The awakening of Naturalism and conscious Individuality, followed, as it was, by the re-birth of the aims and ideals of Antiquity, coincided in its initial stages fairly closely with the turn of the century. The same was true of the next phase of development, when with the leading artists the Renaissance attained its full maturity. This was the case with Giorgione, for example, at Venice, and him we shall therefore exclude from our present selection. At times, however, we shall advance far into the sixteenth century, for it is clear that not infrequently the turning-point of artistic progress lies beyond the line of rigid classification.

Whatever the fame, say, of Mantegna or Bellini, the early North Italian Schools do not enjoy a reputation equal to that of the contemporary Schools of Middle Italy. After the coming of Giorgione and Titian this, no doubt, ceases to be true; in fact the pre-eminence of Venice is then as generally admitted as ever that of Florence during the fifteenth century. But for the period under consideration it is evident that public opinion still shares that strong partiality for the arts of Tuscany and Umbria which is manifested so clearly in the *Lives* of Vasari. This is not the place to discuss for what reasons, and in what measure, that preference had its justification, and has it doubtless still, though we can now survey the whole Renaissance period from the vantage-point of a later era. But in passing we may at least recall how many of Vasari's estimates were the expression of personal prejudice, dictated by a narrow sense of sectional loyalty or, more justifiably, by that preference for an art of kindred aims to his own, which is evinced by every judge himself an artist. Considering then what far-reaching influence has been exerted by Vasari's writings ever since their first appearance, it seems quite probable that there is still a trace of his personal bias in the current opinions of to-day.

At all events, whereas Florentine drawings have long been the subject of minute investigation, comparatively little systematic research

6

has as yet been devoted to those of the Schools of Upper Italy.* So far as it is possible to judge, too, the extant material belonging to these latter seems less abundant than might be expected, a fact which could reasonably be interpreted as a sign of neglect on the part of bygone generations. In point of fact, the preservation of drawings, more especially Italian, can only be a matter of chance. By far the most celebrated painter of our present chapter, Giovanni Bellini, will probably always remain comparatively scarce in his drawings, and such men as Crivelli and Borgognone, whose pictures seem so clearly to betray the draughtsman's vision, provide even more striking examples of unaccountable scarcity. It may be well here to remark that our selection of plates aims primarily at giving a broad and general survey, and that this, in a volume of limited size, will necessarily entail a very incomplete treatment of the artists whose drawings have survived in greater numbers. A case in point will be Carpaccio, while among the earlier masters Pisanello and Jacopo Bellini will suffer equally.

Even Pisanello's forerunners, whose style is marked by its close formal affinity with that of Franco-Flemish illuminators, have left a considerable quantity of drawings. Not a few of these can still be ascribed to known artists. Thus one may readily recognise the hand of STEFANO DA VERONA (1393–1450/1), whose signature appears on an " Adoration," dated 1435, at Milan, in a number of pen sketches of a curious loose texture; and the same applies, though with less certainty, to Stefano's Lombard contemporaries, MICHELINO DA BESOZZO, the author of a small signed panel at Siena, and the brothers Zavattari, who painted the frescoes in the Theodalinda Chapel at Monza. In the case of Giovannino de' Grassi, an artist of a somewhat older generation, there is even a sheet attested as his by a contemporary inscription in the charming volume of studies preserved at Bergamo. Another drawing in this book claims special interest for

---

* Since the completion of this book, the excellent volume of " *Venezianische Zeichnungen des Quattrocento* " (1925), by Detlev von Hadeln, has appeared. It is referred to in the ensuing catalogue of plates, but the latter were selected independently of it.

being connected with an illumination in the Limbourg brothers' *Très Riches Heures*, at Chantilly. Here we touch the very root of the most important problem of North Italian painting prior to the advent of Mantegna; but, unfortunately, the evidence is not conclusive, and in the end it remains doubtful in what relation the Lombard and French artists stood to each other. For the present, therefore, the origins of Pisanello's style are obscure. It may be worth mentioning, however, that Gentile da Fabriano, an Umbrian artist allied to Pisanello, has been shown to derive in all his essential characteristics from his older townsmen, such as Alegretto Nuzzi. It is quite possible, therefore, that the factor of French influence was not really of such importance with the Veronese master as has been supposed, and that apparent imitation may simply be due to the fact that Pisanello's art sprang from a similar courtly *milieu* as that in which the French illuminators were formed.

ANTONIO PISANO, called Pisanello (1397–1455), was considerably younger than his Veronese townsman Stefano, and, combining greater endowments with a more developed sense of naturalism, he rose to be one of the protagonists of the Renaissance in Upper Italy. Much of his present-day fame he owes to his activity as a medallist, but during his lifetime his reputation as a painter was probably even greater, and he had certainly come into it at an earlier date. Unfortunately his frescoes painted in collaboration with Gentile da Fabriano at Venice, and others executed in the Lateran, at Rome, have vanished; the first of his extant works is the " Annunciation " in S. Fermo at Verona, while his splendid " St. George," in S. Anastasia, is evidently somewhat later in date. Of his easel pictures only the portraits at Bergamo and Paris, and the " SS. Antony and George," in the National Gallery, are undisputed. His popular " St. Eustace," also in London, has, on the other hand, been thought by certain authorities to be the work of a skilful disciple. Many of the drawings in the celebrated *Recueil Vallardi* are certainly by pupils or imitators, but even discounting these, there remain close upon a hundred originals. Some characteristic specimens are included among our plates, and will bear witness both to the singular charm of Pisanello's art and its conscious striving after new aims.

An equally prominent place among the early fifteenth-century draughtsmen belongs to Pisanello's Venetian contemporary, JACOPO BELLINI (*c.* 1400–1470), a disciple of Gentile da Fabriano. As an original and complete collection, his two celebrated sketch-books, now preserved in the British Museum and the Louvre, constitute, indeed, a document of almost unique importance. Little survives of Jacopo's work as a painter. There is a fine figure of "Christ on the Cross" in the Verona Gallery, and a few small pictures of a votive type may be seen at Florence, Lovere, and elsewhere. But though they reveal a freshness of vision similar to Pisanello's, and a devoutness that anticipates the sentiment of the later Venetians, these works convey no adequate impression of Bellini's artistic capacity, and fail to compensate for the loss of his frescoes painted at Verona, Padua, and Venice. The singular importance of the two sketch-books is due in no small measure to the fact that they help to fill this gap in the artist's work. As opposed to the Vallardi drawings which are mainly devoted to the naturalistic study of single figures, they contain a quantity of elaborate compositions which enable one to form a clear opinion of Bellini's skill in grouping and of his sense of spatial relations. It has been pointed out that the absence of Venetian motifs is a feature common to both the volumes, and one that is particularly significant since the artist bestows great attention to his architectural settings and landscape backgrounds. This provides a valuable clue to the date of the drawings, and makes it probable that they belong to about the year 1440, when Bellini was working at the court of Ferrara.

That Jacopo Bellini, despite the newness of his striving, ranges with the precursors of the Renaissance rather than with its exponents proper, becomes clear on proceeding to the great Paduan painter and engraver, ANDREA MANTEGNA (1431–1506). While Bellini never completely freed himself from the shackles of mediæval tradition, Mantegna emerged from his earliest beginnings as an artist of an altogether modern type. To Francesco Squarcione is given the credit of being

Mantegna's actual teacher, but the few surviving pictures of this artist are of a mediocrity hard to reconcile with his reputation, and one has to search further to trace the decisive influences in the formation of his pupil's genius. True, Mantegna may well have derived from him his first impulse to the study of the Antique; but there can be little doubt that both Jacopo Bellini and Niccolò Pizzolo, a somewhat older painter of the Paduan group, exerted far more telling influence on him, and that even they were subordinate as compared with Donatello. Though working in different materials, the great Florentine was clearly the chief inspirer of Mantegna's youth; from him he derived the real fundamentals of his art: his sculptural solidity in the rendering of form, his science of perspective and spatial recession, and above all his sense of the monumental. It is usual to lay stress on the pagan spirit of Mantegna's genius, and no doubt this constitutes a real characteristic of a number of his Mantuan productions, the frescoes, for example, in the Castello di Corte, the "Great Triumph of Cæsar," now at Hampton Court, or the splendid allegories painted for the *Studiolo* of his patroness, Isabella Gonzaga. Nevertheless it would be a grave error to deny that the artist compassed a profound religious sentiment in many of his easel pictures and, for that matter, in his early frescoes in the Eremitani at Padua. Though perhaps less obvious and easy to analyse than his leanings to Humanism, the mystic side of Mantegna's genius is yet of great importance for his right understanding.

Among the numerous minor painters who, like Mantegna, issued from the School of Francesco Squarcione, the most generally interesting was MARCO ZOPPO (*c.* 1433–1498). A native of Bologna, he came to Padua in 1453, and after serving his apprenticeship in that city, worked alternately at Venice and in the town of his birth. Besides assimilating the characteristics of the Paduan School, Zoppo seems also to have felt the influence of Cossa. But while he thus drew his style from potent sources, Zoppo never attained to the inner power of a really great master. Indeed, his art is rather one of blunt realism than of forcible severity; it is harsh without carrying the conviction of genuine asceticism. Zoppo's most ambitious production now existing is a

" Virgin Enthroned," at Berlin, which, as an inscription records, was painted at Venice in 1471. A work of fine decorative quality, it yet shows him to less advantage than certain smaller panels, which are well exemplified with the " Pietà " of the National Gallery, and the " Madonna " of the Cook Collection at Richmond. After Zoppo, our attention is chiefly claimed by the Dalmatian, GIORGIO SCHIAVONE (b. 1435), who entered Squarcione's studio some years later than the Bolognese artist, subsequently returned to his native country, and is last heard of in 1474, when he was again residing at Padua. It has been supposed that Schiavone had a share in the frescoes of the Ovetari Chapel, but as these were already finished in 1452, this seems impossible for simple reasons of chronology. Of his easel-pictures the " SS. Jerome and Alexius," in the Bergamo Gallery, and the " Virgin and Child " at Canford Manor, show strong resemblance to the style of Zoppo, and indeed both have in the past been attributed to the latter. As a rule, however, Schiavone's handling is somewhat coarser and more angular, and many of his figures are mannered and ill-drawn. Like Crivelli, he never tired of introducing garlands and festoons of fruit into his compositions, and this is perhaps the most attractive feature of his work. The National Gallery is fortunate in possessing two of the best specimens of his art; both the larger polyptych and smaller " Madonna " combine a meticulous finish with pleasing decorative effects. The last of this group of painters calling for mention is BERNARDO DA PARENZA (c. 1460–1531), who is known to have worked as an assistant of Mantegna. The best of his easel-pictures are now in the Doria Palace at Rome, while some frescoes belonging to the latter end of his career are preserved in the cloisters of S. Giustina at Padua. At his best Parentino reveals himself as an artist of considerable skill and vivacity, and though his language of form has still much in common with the closer followers of Squarcione, he also clearly benefited from the example of Mantegna, and had acquaintance besides with Ercole de' Roberti. Like Zoppo and Schiavone he does not merit the honours of a great master, but shares the historical interest attaching to the other members of the Squarcionesque group.

By dealing with Zoppo along with the minor Paduans, we have already touched the School of the Emilia, though not its most important centre of painting at the period here under consideration. So far as the fifteenth century is concerned, it was Ferrara, the seat of the Estensian court, where artistic activity was greatest. Among the first to produce work of a higher order were Bono and Oriolo, two disciples of Pisanello; but of them it will suffice to say that they paved the way for the coming of Cosimo Tura (1430–1495). It was he who, to all intents and purposes, opened the great period of Ferrarese painting that covered the reigns of Borso and Ercole I, and he, moreover, who brought the early school of the Emilia to its zenith. Like Zoppo, Tura in his youth must have been in touch with Padua; broadly speaking, his art sprang from the same sources as Mantegna's, partly, no doubt, from Mantegna's itself, while probably the great Umbrian, Piero della Francesca, was also in some measure responsible for its formation. But if the monumental character of Tura's style can be traced to certain outside influences, his art was yet imbued with qualities so essentially his own that he undoubtedly ranked with the most distinctive personalities of the Renaissance. In the whole range of fifteenth-century painting there is little to compare with the intense emotional force that he compassed; and with this inward power he combined a bigness of design and sumptuousness of colour which proclaim him a master of very high accomplishment. Tura's science of perspective, his bold foreshortenings, and the metallic hardness of his rendering of form are features occurring also in the work of his townsman, Francesco Cossa (c. 1438–1477). His frescoes belonging to the cycle of symbolical compositions in the Schifanoia Palace at Ferrara, and certain easel-pictures, such as the superb "Virgin with Saints" in the Bologna Gallery, bespeak an artist of more balanced and harmonious temperament than Tura, while, in point of style, they show closer acquaintance with Piero della Francesca. Of the few available data bearing on Cossa's life, his period of residence at Bologna calls for mention, as he was doubtless at that time an agent in establishing the sway of Ferrarese art both in the city of the Bentivoglio and at Modena. It may be interesting to add that while working at Bologna, Cossa's activity included the designing of stained-glass windows for churches, specimens of which have survived in S. Giovanni in Monte, in the André Collection at Paris, and at Berlin.

From Tura and Cossa we proceed to a somewhat younger Ferrarese artist, ERCOLE DE' ROBERTI (c. 1455–1496), who in many of his works attained to a style of great dramatic vigour, and showed remarkable qualities as a colourist. It is probable that in his youth Roberti was apprenticed to one or other of his older townsmen, but there is also abundant evidence of Mantegna's influence in his work, and, to a less degree, of the Bellini. During the 'eighties Roberti is known to have worked at Ravenna and Bologna, when he produced, among other things, the great altar-panel in the Brera, now generally considered his masterpiece, and the spirited predella-pictures of the Dresden and Liverpool Galleries, which are of special interest to us as several studies for them have been preserved. After returning to Ferrara in 1486 and succeeding Tura as the court-painter of the Estensi, Roberti's style underwent considerable changes, his forms becoming ampler and more rounded, thereby linking up with the early manner of Costa. To the latter, indeed, Roberti's " Concert " in the National Gallery was at one time seriously attributed. Opinion no longer differs on this particular work ; but generally speaking the end of Roberti's production still presents some points of uncertainty, particularly as regards its border-line to that of another painter, Ercole Grandi, the disciple of Costa whom Vasari mistook for his greater namesake. To Grandi is generally given the Strozzi altar-panel of the " Virgin Enthroned " in the National Gallery, though a slight element of doubt still lingers about this attribution. Grandi's claim on the charming " St. George " of the Corsini Gallery has, on the other hand, now definitely been rejected in favour of FRANCESCO FRANCIA (c. 1450–1517), of Bologna.

The name of Francia is chiefly associated with his numerous later Madonnas and " Sante Conversazione " which in their somewhat sentimental character, approximate to the Umbrian manner of Perugino. His early pictures, however, which date back to the 'eighties and are

13

paintings, it is true, shared the fate of Gentile's, but in his altar-pieces his development can be followed, step by step, from his Mantegnesque beginnings to the point at which he links up with Giorgione and Titian. We cannot, of course, enumerate the individual works that mark the course of this extraordinary development, nor attempt to analyse the genius capable of such transformation as that which separates the Brera " Pietà " from the matchless altar in S. Zaccharia. Few artists have compassed so wide a range of emotion as his, embracing, as it does, the Paduan austerity of his youth and the tender pathos of his maturity and old age. Nothing is more opposed to this gradual advance than the abruptness with which Mantegna emerged, a finished artist in his earliest productions. A fundamental difference of mind no doubt accounts for this in the main; but certainly in Bellini's greater versatility the factor of technical progress is also involved. For if the sharp linearity of his early work changed by degrees into fused modelling and colourism, there is no question but that this was largely due to his adopting the new oil-medium as used by Antonello. To what degree Antonello himself was the originator of Bellini's technical experiments, is hard to say. It is now known that oils were in use at Venice before the date of the Sicilian's arrival, and it is probable, therefore, that his methods were not really so revolutionary as was formerly thought. His incomparably greater skill in handling the new medium should not, however, be forgotten, and if, historically, the most important phase of Bellini's development was from about 1475–85, there is not the least doubt that it was from Antonello that he was then deriving his strongest impulse.

A satisfactory grouping of the minor Venetians belonging to the final stages of the Quattrocento is no easy matter, since these artists may be observed to change their models repeatedly, and to exercise a certain mutual influence upon each other. Their chief inspirer was, needless to say, Giovanni Bellini, but it would be wrong to suppose that all the " Bellinesques " issued directly from his studio, or even that they owed stimulus to him alone. Before proceeding, a few words must be said of the older Muranese group, though as yet no drawings can be attributed to either of its leaders, Antonio and Bartolomeo Vivarini. To them, however, and notably to Antonio's son ALVISE VIVARINI (c. 1450–1505), a distinct artistic current may be traced, which, while commingling strongly with that of the Bellini, retained in some measure a style and character of its own. The competition, and even rivalry, thought to have existed between the successive generations of the Bellini and Vivarini has, on the whole, been overstated; but in Alvise the Muranese School produced an artist of at least comparable merit to the Venetian, his " Resurrection " in S. Giovanni in Bragora being a striking, though isolated, proof of his power. Among his disciples, too, Alvise could boast of such men as Basaiti, Lotto, and Palma, and his influence was likewise felt in the mysterious painter and engraver, JACOPO DE BARBARI (c. 1450–1515), who played a *rôle* of some importance in the life of Dürer. Let us add that Crivelli, a painter of marked individuality who practised chiefly in the Marches, derived from the same group of older Muranese artists as did Alvise, and retained their style of a yet strongly Byzantine character until close upon the turn of the century. LAZZARO BASTIANI, again, though not an artist of a higher order, had a school and following of his own, and was responsible for the training of such men as MANSUETI and BENEDETTO DIANA, and even, in the opinion of some, of Carpaccio. There remain, of course, a host of direct disciples of Bellini, quite apart from those whose work belongs to the mature period of Venetian painting. Among the older ones, VINCENZO CATENA and FRANCESCO BISSOLO were perhaps the most competent, but we shall not pause to consider them individually, and indeed their historical importance is comparatively small.

Much more distinguished painters, each in his way, were CIMA DA CONEGLIANO (1460–1518) and VITTORE CARPACCIO (c. 1455–1527). They have no particular bond in common, but the fact that their respective positions in the history of Venetian art offers an interesting contrast, will justify their here being dealt with together. A native of Friuli, Cima is thought to have had connections with Vicenza in his early stages, and to have settled at Venice about the beginning of the 'nineties. As a matter of fact, it is hard to believe that he was trained elsewhere than at Venice, for while the vigorous character of his art and his love of landscape bear witness to his extraction from the people of the hill-country, he at an early date commanded a bigness of style and a brilliancy of colour in which no trace of provincial schooling is visible. In the ranks of the Bellinesques, Cima's position is that of a great master. The point, however, in which he differs so strikingly from Carpaccio is that, despite his power, his name stands for no achievement specifically his own. Carpaccio, in point of absolute ability, was probably of a lower order. Working, though he did, till long after the death of Giorgione, he lacked much of the freedom and stateliness of the Friulan master. In his special field, however, that of narrative compositions, he is without a rival. Since Ruskin's days, his various cycles, painted for the schools of certain religious confraternities, have received almost as much attention as the loftiest creations of Bellini himself. Their charm is irresistible; no painter has more endearing qualities than the eager narrative and inexhaustible store of anecdote that are characteristic of Carpaccio. Without detracting from their worth, it must be admitted, however, that their prominence to-day is in some measure accidental, and due to the fact that time has dealt so severely with the works of Gentile. No matter whose pupil he was,—we need not dwell on this doubtful point— Carpaccio's debt to the elder of the Bellini brothers can have been no less evident than that of Cima to the younger.

Turning to a brief examination of the art-centres of the Venetian *terra-ferma*, we should recall the pre-eminence of Verona in the early part of the century, and that of Padua at a subsequent date. On proceeding to a yet later phase of Quattrocento painting, we have chiefly to bestow our attention on the Vicentine School. Not that Vicenza had risen to a position of leadership comparable to that of Verona or Padua in former times; but in BARTOLOMEO MONTAGNA (*c.* 1455–1524) it produced a painter of quite unusual merit among provincials. That he owed much to the Venetians is readily perceptible, while the influence of Mantegna may clearly be felt in a certain austerity of sentiment and expression. Perhaps his masterpiece is the Brera " Virgin Enthroned,"

18

a picture deriving an air of such monumentality from its effective massing and virile drawing, that it bears comparison with the finest productions of the North Italian Quattrocento. A disciple of Montagna, GIOVANNI BUONCONSIGLIO (c. 1470–1535), was also the author of some impressive compositions. His "Pietà" in the Vicenza Gallery is, in particular, a work of great beauty. His standard, however, was not nearly so consistently high as Montagna's, while GIOVANNI SPERANZA, another of the Vicentines, seldom, if ever, rose above mediocrity. Among the Paduan masters contemporary to Montagna, we need only mention FRANCESCO BONSIGNORI (? 1455–1519), who, under the inspiration of Mantegna, showed considerable power as a portraitist. Of the Veronese it will be enough to name FRANCESCO MORONE (? 1470–1529), an artist of delicate charm in his representations of the Virgin, and his robuster townsman LIBERALE, who, strange to say, started his career as an illuminator. As to the Brescians and Bergamasques, it was not until a later date that they came into prominence, the generation of Romanino and Moretto being the first to give real celebrity to those schools.

There remains to trace the development of the Lombard School from the stage at which it was represented by the Zavattari and Michelino, artists who were mentioned at the outset of our survey. To link up with these primitives we have to revert to about the middle of the fifteenth century, when in Lombardy, as elsewhere, a more realistic and modern style was coming into being. Though perhaps not the first representative of this movement, it is VINCENZO FOPPA (1427–1515), a native of Brescia, who emerges as its earliest exponent of a marked personality, and he thus holds a somewhat similar place in Milanese painting to that of Tura at Ferrara. His earliest dated picture is a " Crucifixion " of 1456, at Bergamo, a work showing him in a yet immature phase and apparently influenced by Jacopo Bellini. Quite a different idea of Foppa's power is given by his impressive " Adoration " in the National Gallery, which must have been executed some time during the 'nineties. That Bramante, the great Umbrian painter and architect who was then residing at Milan, left his impress strongly his acquaintance with Antonello in works such as his " Virgin with Saints," in the Brera. The " Christ at the Column " of the Cook Collection is indeed a case where it is hard to decide between the rival claims of the two masters. The celebrated " Ecce Homo " already belongs to the Leonardesque phase of Solario's development, but one in which a remnant of Foppesque style is still clearly perceptible. His later style became more purely Leonardesque, and was followed in the end by a phase of curious affinity to certain Netherlandish mannerists working under Milanese influence. As a portrait painter Solario ranges with the best of his time, and this may likewise be said of his townsman BOLTRAFFIO (1467–1517). The latter in his religious compositions appears as an artist somewhat languid in spirit and lacking in invention, but there is no denying a certain dignity in his style and a fine quality of finish in all his autograph works. The " Madonna di Casio," in the Louvre, is perhaps his greatest achievement.

The younger followers of Leonardo belong, both in point of time and style, to the chapter of Cinquecento painting. If the development of Milanese art under these later painters were generally characteristic of the North Italian Schools, it would be hard to deny that the Quattrocento took an inglorious end. As a matter of fact, the School of Milan forms quite an exception. Nothing was more opposed to its rapid decline than the steady growth of the Venetian School; nor did the later artists of the Emilia belie their promises as did the Milanese. At Ferrara, Dosso Dossi and Garofalo sustained a noble tradition; there came Correggio at Parma, one of the greatest masters of all time; and Bologna, too, during the second half of the century, saw the rise of new artistic ideals which, though not without certain inherent failings, gained world-wide dominance in their time. At Genoa, finally, a school of painting came into being which raised Liguria to a leading place among the provinces of art. Thus the North Italian Quattrocento, taken in its entirety, may be said to merge into another equally great era, and to have a claim to interest over and above that of its actual achievement.

CATALOGUE OF THE PLATES

ANONYMOUS, NORTH ITALIAN (*c.* 1400).

1. ST. JAMES THE GREATER. Paris (Louvre). Brush on blue-grey prepared paper, 258 × 114 mm. There is a study of the Virgin and Child enthroned on the back.

ANONYMOUS, LOMBARD SCHOOL (*c.* 1410–1420).

2. THE NATIVITY. Milan (Ambrosiana). Pen and bistre wash on vellum, radius *c.* 80 mm. See P. Toesca: *La Pittura e la Miniatura nella Lombardia*, Milan, 1912, p. 450.

STYLE OF MICHELINO DA BESOZZO.

3. STANDING FIGURE OF ST. PETER. Paris (Louvre). Water-colours (yellow, light blue and light green) on vellum, 190 × 128 mm. One of a set of four sheets representing Apostles. Two are reproduced by Toesca, op. cit., p. 443.

STEFANO DA VERONA (1393–1450/1).

4. STUDY FOR A FIGURE OF A PROPHET. London (British Museum). Pen and bistre, 232 × 210 mm. There is a similar figure on the back. Reproduced by the *Vasari Society*, IV, 13–14. Other drawings by the same hand are at Paris, Florence, and Dresden. See *L'Arte*, IV, p. 238; X, p. 374; XXV, p. 112.

ANTONIO PISANO, called PISANELLO (1397–1455).

5. STUDIES OF A HORSE. Paris (Louvre). Pen and ink on paper, 165 × 142 mm. Recueil Vallardi, 2468, fol. 277. Z. von Manteuffel: *Die Gemälde und Zeichnungen des Antonio Pisano*, Halle, 1909, p. 128. Observe the slit nostrils.

6. DESIGN FOR A MEDAL. Paris (Louvre). Pen and bistre, 165 ×
142 mm. Inscribed " Pisani Pictoris Opus." Recueil
Vallardi, 2486, fol. 249. The arms are those of Alfonso of
Aragon. G. F. Hill : *Pisanello* (Duckworth's Library of Art),
1903, p. 204. Manteuffel, op. cit., pp. 128–9. (Photo
Giraudon.)

7. STUDY OF TWO YOKED OXEN. Paris (Louvre). Silver-point
and brush on vellum, retouched in places, 145 × 205 mm.
Recueil Vallardi, 2409, fol. 202. There is a slight sketch of
a horse on the back. Manteuffel, op. cit., p. 125. (Photo
Giraudon.)

SCHOOL OF VERONA (*c.* 1440).

8. A RIDER ON A REARING HORSE. Collection of Mr. Henry
Oppenheimer, London. Pen and ink, 255 × 180 mm.
There is a sketch of the embalming of a corpse on the back.
Recalls Pisanello in treatment and Jacopo Bellini in subject.
Compare the following.

JACOPO BELLINI (*c.* 1400–1470/1).

9. ST. GEORGE AND THE DRAGON. London (British Museum).
Silver-point, 300 × 240 mm. Fol. 7a of sketch-book.
Goloubew : *Les Dessins de Jacopo Bellini*, Brussels, 1912, I, 8.
On fol. 6b the princess is represented kneeling before the
castle walls.

10. HEAD OF A MAN IN PROFILE. Paris (Louvre). Silver-point on
bluish prepared vellum, *c.* 350 × 175 mm. Fol. 22a of sketch-
book. The outlines slightly retouched. Goloubew, II, 20.
On Bellini's drawings in general, cf. *Rassegna d'Arte*, IX
(1909), p. 55, and *Graphische Künste (Mitteilungen)*, 1916,
p. 41. (Photo Giraudon.)

11. CHRIST IN LIMBO. Paris (Louvre). Silver-point on bluish prepared vellum, *c.* 350 × 240 mm. Fol. 21b of sketch-book. Goloubew, II, 19. The drawing was used for a predella-picture at Padua (Galleria Comunale, No. 410). (Photo Giraudon.)

12. THE ASCENSION. London (British Museum). Lead-point; *c.* 300 × 245 mm. Fol. 59b of sketch-book. Goloubew, I, 68. Slightly retouched. The landscape extends to left over the preceding page. For the technique of the London sketch-book, cf. Meder, *Die Handzeichnung* (Vienna, 1919), pp. 75–6.

ANDREA MANTEGNA (1431–1506).

13. THE VIRGIN AND CHILD. London (British Museum). Pen and bistre, 197 × 139 mm. Dates from the artist's middle period; cf. Berenson: *Study and Criticism*, 2nd Series, p. 52. For a subtle analysis of Mantegna's mind, cf. R. Fry in the *Burlington Magazine*, VIII (1905), p. 87.

14. THE CALUMNY OF APELLES. London (British Museum). Pen and bistre, 205 × 380 mm. Engraved by Mocetto (Hind 9). For an explanation of the subject cf. Förster in *Jahrbuch der pr. Kunstsammlungen*, VIII (1887), p. 29.

SCHOOL OF ANDREA MANTEGNA.

15. THE CRUCIFIXION. London (British Museum). Pen and brush in bistre, heightened with white, on grey paper, 240 × 215 mm. C. Brun (*Zeitschrift für bildende Kunst*, XVI, p. 119): Study for the S. Zeno predella (Louvre); Morelli (*Kunstchronik*, III, p. 526): School of Foppa. Mantegna's composition derived from a lost fresco by Jacopo Bellini at Verona. Compare also the predella by Zenale and Butinone at Treviglio.

16. TRITONS WITH SEA-HORSES. Paris (Ecole des Beaux-Arts). Pen, 170 × 250 mm. Engraved in Ottley's *School of Design*, 1823, p. 15. (Weigel: *Die Werke der Meister in ihren Handzeichnungen*, 1865, No. 4578.)

17. ST. JEROME. Berlin (Kupferstichkabinet der Staatlichen Museen). Pen, 171 × 136 mm. By an artist resembling in style the engravers of the Mantegna School. Cf. Borenius: *Four Italian Engravers*, 1923, pp. 27–54.

MARCO ZOPPO (*c.* 1433–1498).

18. STUDIES OF THE VIRGIN AND CHILD. Munich (Graphische Sammlung). Pen and wash, 288 × 196 mm. There are similar studies on the back. Cf. *Vasari Society*, II, 15–16, and *Frankfurt Drawings Publ.*, IX, 5–6.

GIORGIO SCHIAVONE (*b.* 1435).

19. HEAD OF A MAN IN PROFILE. Paris (Musée Jacquemart-André). Water-colours on vellum, 350 × 250 mm. Signed " Opus Schavoni Dalmatici Squarzoni." The only known work of this type by Schiavone. It is on the border between a finished picture and a drawing. (Photo Bulloz.)

BERNARDO PARENTINO (*c.* 1460–1531).

20. ALLEGORY OF A ROMAN TRIUMPH. London (British Museum). Pen and ink, 244 × 208 mm. There are two similar drawings at Christ Church, Oxford (Colvin, II, 29–30).

COSIMO TURA (1430–1495).

21. THE VIRGIN AND CHILD WITH SAINTS. London (British Museum). Pen and bistre, 105 × 213 mm. Repeatedly inscribed " horo " (gold). For the reconstruction of a similar altar-piece, now scattered, see *Rassegna d'Arte*, V (1905), pp. 145–6. Nos. 772 and 3070 of the National Gallery offer analogies for the shell and dolphin ornaments.

22. HERCULES KILLING THE LION. Formerly Emile Wauters Collection, Paris. Brush in bistre, heightened with white, 210 × 150 mm. Inscribed "Gosme." Formerly in the Valori Collection. F. Lees: *The Art of the Great Masters*, 1913, fig. 7. Sold at Amsterdam in June, 1926 (No. 196). There are similar figures on the throne of the Berlin "Madonna with two Saints."

23. THE INFANT CHRIST. Collection of Mr. Henry Oppenheimer, London. Pen and bistre with water-colours, 93 × 84 mm. The Child in front of the draped curtain accords closely, but in reverse, with the corresponding figure of a picture at Bergamo (Academia Carrara, No. 263).

STYLE OF FRANCESCO COSSA.

24. VENUS EMBRACING CUPID. Collection of Mr. E. Holland. Pen and bistre, 282 × 396 mm. Apparently derived from the Schifanoia frescoes. *Vasari Society*, II, 14. For other drawings attributed to Cossa, see *Vasari Society*, 2nd Series, II, 1, and Fairfax Murray publication, plate 92.

ERCOLE DE' ROBERTI (*c.* 1455–1496).

25. THE BETRAYAL OF CHRIST. Florence (Uffizi). Pen and bistre, 150 × 217 mm. Sketch for the predella-picture from S. Giovanni in Monte, Bologna, now in the Dresden Gallery. See below, No. 26.

26. PIETÀ. London (British Museum). Brush, heightened with white (much oxydized) on yellow prepared surface, 211 × 213 mm. Sketch for the Liverpool predella-picture. A similar drawing of the Figure of Christ (? copy) is at Berlin; cf. *Archivio Storico dell' Arte*, II (1889), p. 347. The composition was adapted (in reverse) by Lodovico Mazzolino for his picture, now in the collection of Sir Herbert Cook (No. 542; from the Weber Collection).

27. HEAD OF A WOMAN CRYING OUT. Collection of Mr. Pierpont Morgan, New York. Charcoal, *c.* 260 × 190 mm. Probably the study for a head in a " Massacre of the Innocents." Fairfax Murray publication, IV, 30, as of the Lombard School.

STYLE OF ERCOLE DE' ROBERTI.

28. STUDY FOR A FIGURE OF THE PLANET MERCURY. Bayonne (Musée Bonnat). Pen and bistre, 240 × 170 mm. In the Bonnat publication (1924) as by Domenico Campagnola. The vigorous action is very reminiscent of Roberti.

LORENZO COSTA (*c.* 1460–1535).

29. STUDY OF AN OLD MAN'S HEAD. Berlin (Kupferstichkabinet der Staatlichen Museen). Brush, heightened with white on grey prepared paper, 316 × 193 mm. Possibly for the head of God the Father in the altar-piece in S. Martino at Bologna.

30. ALLEGORICAL FIGURE OF FORTUNE. Berlin (Kupferstichkabinet der Staatlichen Museen). Brush, heightened with white on grey prepared paper, 316 × 193 mm. Reverse side of preceding drawing.

31. STUDY OF FEMALE FIGURES ADORING. London (British Museum). Pen and ink, 115 × 105 mm. Probably a study for attendant figures in a Crucifixion. On reverse the study of a hand. Collections : Charles I, Lankrink, Lely, Esdaile, Bale.

FRANCESCO FRANCIA (*c.* 1450–1517).

32. THE ANNUNCIATION WITH ATTENDANT SAINTS. Paris (Louvre). Brush, heightened with white, 275 × 195 mm. Resembles the composition of the " Franciscan " Annunciation by Francia, painted in 1500 for the SS. Annunziata, now in the Bologna Gallery (No. 371).

28

FRANCESCO ZAGANELLI (1465–1531).

33. STUDIES FOR A MADONNA. Stockholm (National Museum). Brush in bistre, 250 × 178 mm. Drawn from waxed draperies over a lay-figure; see Meder: *Die Handzeichnung*, etc., p. 443. Sirén (*Italienska Handteckningar*, p. 116) points out the connection with a picture at Chantilly; but cf. also Brera, Nos. 455 and 458.

MELOZZO DA FORLI (1438–1494).

34. HEAD OF CHRIST IN FORESHORTENING. London (British Museum). Charcoal, 390 × 260 mm. Pricked for transfer. Study for the fresco in SS. Apostoli at Rome. See Schmarsow: *Melozzo da Forli* (1886), pp. 368–9. A study of angels, also in the British Museum, supposed to be another sketch for these frescoes, is by Liberale da Verona.

ANTONELLO DA MESSINA (1430–1479).

35. PORTRAIT OF A YOUTH. Vienna (Albertina). Charcoal, 335 × 273 mm. Formerly attributed to Bellini and Bonsignori; first recognised by A. Venturi as Antonello (*L'Arte*, XXIV (1921), p. 71).

GENTILE BELLINI (1429–1507).

36. A TURKISH WOMAN SEATED. London (British Museum). Pen, 214 × 176 mm. Inscribed " Oro," " argento," " rosso," etc. This sheet and its companion (also B.M.), along with copies of similar figures at Paris and Frankfurt, were used by Pinturicchio for frescoes in the Apartamenta Borgia in the Vatican. See *L'Arte*, I (1898), p. 32.

37. SELF-PORTRAIT. Berlin (Kupferstichkabinet der Staatlichen Museen). Black chalk, 230 × 195 mm. Pricked for transfer. Study for the " Procession before St. Mark's " in the Venice Academy. Lippmann-Grote, I, 73.

GIOVANNI MANSUETI (1470–1530).

38. A MIRACLE OF THE CROSS. Florence (Uffizi). Pen in bistre, 442 × 519 mm. Attributed by D. v. Hadeln to Gentile Bellini (*Venezianische Zeichnungen des Quattrocento*, 1925, p. 45), but we yet incline to think that the connection with No. 564 of the Venice Academy by Mansueti is closer. (Photo Allinari.)

GIOVANNI BELLINI (*c.* 1435–1516).

39. STUDY OF A MAN SEATED. Collection of Mr. A. G. B. Russell, London. Pen on reddish tinted paper, 185 × 140 mm. From the Banks and Poynter Collections. See Borenius in the *Connoisseur*, LXVI (1923), p. 5. *Vasari Society*, 2nd Series, VII (1926), plate 3.

40. STUDIES FOR A FIGURE OF THE BAPTIST. Collection of Mr. J. Böhler, Lucerne. Pen, 147 × 146 mm. Joined together with another sheet of studies by Bellini, reproduced by Hadeln, op. cit., plate 57.

41. FIGURE OF AN APOSTLE. Bayonne (Musée Bonnat). Pen, *c.* 150 × 90 mm. A similar figure of St. Peter, also at Bayonne, is reproduced in the Bonnat publication, II (1925), plate 10, attributed to Ercole de' Roberti.

FOLLOWER OF GIOVANNI BELLINI.

42. PIETÀ. London (British Museum). Pen and bistre wash, 130 × 95 mm. Inscribed above in a later hand " Udini," which refers probably to Giovanni Martini da Udine. There are studies of children on the back which make an attribution to Martini plausible. A somewhat similar Pietà by Martini is the picture in the Walters Collection, Baltimore, reproduced in Berenson's *Venetian Painting in America*, plate 94. The composition was probably inspired by the Mond Pietà of Bellini (N.G. 3912).

ALVISE VIVARINI (*c.* 1450–1503/5).

43. STUDIES OF HANDS. Collection of Mr. Frits Lugt, Maartens-
    dijk. Silver-point, heightened with white, on pinkish ground,
    278 × 193 mm. Studies for Vivarini's altar-piece, formerly
    in S. Francesco of Treviso, now in the Venice Academy. See
    Old Master Drawings, Vol. I, No. 1, p. 5.

ALVISE VIVARINI (?).

44. STUDY FOR A FIGURE OF ST. PETER. London (British Museum).
    Body colours over sanguine on paper, 224 × 108 mm. Attri-
    buted by Hadeln to Bellini as the sketch for a lost altar-piece,
    derived from Antonello and engraved by Mocetto (Passavant,
    V, 136, 10). (*Jahrbuch der pr. Kunstsammlungen*, XLV (1924),
    p. 206.) Possibly, however, Vivarini's study *after* Bellini for
    the lost pendant to the St. John the Baptist in the Venice
    Academy. For a drawing in similar technique, cf. Albertina
    publication, 653 (sketch for a picture at Düsseldorf).

FRANCESCO BISSOLO (*op.* 1492–1554).

45. SS. JUSTINA, JOHN THE BAPTIST AND CATHERINE. Venice
    (Academy). Pen and brush, 263 × 200 mm. Formerly
    attributed to Morto da Feltre. First recognised by Gronau
    as the study for an altar-piece by Bissolo at Treviso. Hadeln,
    op. cit., plate 87.

CIMA DA CONEGLIANO (1460–1518).

46. ST. JEROME STANDING. Florence (Uffizi). Brush, heightened
    with white on reddish paper, 230 × 95 mm. Study for the
    altar-piece of 1487 in the Vicenza Gallery (No. 146). See
    Burckhardt: *Cima da Conegliano* (Kunstgeschichtliche Mono-
    graphien, II, Leipzig, 1905), p. 124.

GIOVANNI BUONCONSIGLIO (*c.* 1470–1535).

59. CHRIST AT THE COLUMN. Paris (Louvre). Pen and bistre, 390 × 240 mm. Borenius, op. cit., p. 204, No. 71. (Photo (Giraudon).

FRANCESCO BONSIGNORI (? 1453–1519).

60. PORTRAIT OF GIANFRANCESCO GONZAGA. Florence (Uffizi). Black chalk, *c.* 285 × 215 mm. Connected with a picture in the Bergamo Gallery (No. 399).

FRANCESCO MORONE (*c.* 1470–1529).

61. THE VIRGIN ENTHRONED WITH SAINTS. Florence (Uffizi). Red chalk, 190 × 145 mm. Sketch for a fresco, dated 1515, now in the Verona Gallery (No. 560). A somewhat similar drawing is in the Albertina (Schönbrunner-Meder 181).

LIBERALE DA VERONA (1451–1536).

62. THE PRESENTATION. London (British Museum). Pen and bistre wash, 178 × 147 mm. Identified by Loeser. The angel's types are particularly reminiscent of Liberale. See Venturi, VII (4), p. 799.

VINCENZO FOPPA (1427–1515).

63. THE JUSTICE OF TRAJAN. Berlin (Kupferstichkabinet der Staatlichen Museen). Pen in bistre, 258 × 392 mm. Pricked for transfer. Probably the design for Foppa's fresco in the Medici Bank at Milan. See Ffoulkes and Maiocchi : *Vincenzo Foppa*, New York, 1908, p. 47.

BERNARDINO ZENALE (1436–1526) (?).

64. CHRIST SHOWN TO THE PEOPLE. London (British Museum). Pen and bistre wash, 265 × 183 mm. Inscribed " Zenale " by an old hand. The architecture is very Bramantesque. Also attributed to Bramantino ; see *Bollettino d'Arte*, IX (1915), p. 18.

AMBROGIO BORGOGNONE (*c.* 1460–1523).

65. THE ASSUMPTION OF THE VIRGIN. Berlin (Kupferstichkabinet der Staatlichen Museen). Pen in bistre, 192 × 274 mm. Lippmann-Grote (2nd ed.), No. 53, where a connection with the fresco in S. Simpliciano at Milan is suggested. This is the only known drawing of Borgognone.

AMBROGIO DA PREDIS (? 1450–1520).

66. HEAD OF A YOUTH IN PROFILE. Bayonne (Bonnat Collection). Silver-point, heightened on bluish prepared paper, *c.* 130 × 140 mm. (Plate 11 in the Bonnat publication, I, 1924), as anonymous Lombard. Certainly by Preda. From the Klinkosch Collection.

THE MASTER OF THE ARCHINTO PORTRAIT.

67. STUDY OF A HAND. Milan (Ambrosiana). Silver-point, heightened on bluish prepared paper, *c.* 120 × 130 mm. See *Monatshefte f. Kunstwissenschaft*, XII (1919), p. 262.

BERNARDINO DE' CONTI (*op.* 1496–1522).

68. HEAD OF AN OLD MAN IN PROFILE. Collection of Mr. Henry Oppenheimer, London. Black chalk, *c.* 430 × 275 mm. Compare, for example, Conti's signed portrait of a Cardinal at Berlin (No. 55). Hitherto attributed to Ambrogio da Predis.

Anonymous, North Italian, c. 1400:

St. James the Greater (Louvre)

Anonymous, **Lombard** School, c. 1410/20: The Nativity
(Ambrosiana, Milan)

Style of Michelino da Besozzo: St. Peter (Louvre)

4

Stefano da Verona: Study of a Prophet (British Museum)

Pisanello: Studies of a Horse (Louvre)

Pisanello: Design for a Medal (Louvre)

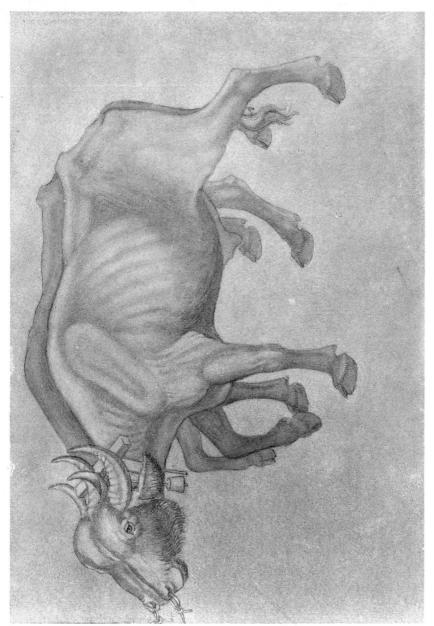

Pisanello: Study of two yoked Oxen (Louvre)

School of Verona: Rider on a rearing Horse
(Coll. Mr. Henry Oppenheimer)

Jacopo Bellini: St. George and the Dragon (British Museum)

Jacopo Bellini: Head of a Man in Profile (Louvre)

Jacopo Bellini: Christ in Limbo (Louvre)

Jacopo Bellini: The Ascension (British Museum)

Andrea Mantegna: Virgin and Child (British Museum)

Andrea Mantegna: The Calumny of Apelles (British Museum)

School of Mantegna: The Crucifixion (British Museum)

School of Mantegna: Tritons with Sea-Horses
(Ecole des Beaux-Arts, Paris)

School of Mantegna: St. Jerome (Berlin Print-Room)

Marco Zoppo: Studies for **Virgin** and Child (Munich Print-Room)

Giorgio Schiavone: Portrait of a Man (Musée Jacquemart-André, Paris)

Bernardo Parentino: Allegory of a Roman Triumph
(British Museum)

Cosimo Tura: Virgin and Child with Saints (British Museum)

Cosimo Tura: Hercules killing the Lion
(formerly Wauters Coll., Paris)

Cosimo Tura: The Infant Christ
(Coll. Mr. Henry Oppenheimer)

Style of Francesco Cossa: Venus embracing Cupid
(Coll. Mr. E. Holland)

Ercole de' Roberti: The Betrayal of Christ (Uffizi, Florence)

Ercole de' Roberti: Pietà (British Museum)

Ercole de' Roberti: Head of a Woman crying out
(Coll. Mr. P. Morgan)

Style of Ercole de' Roberti: Figure of Mercury (Bayonne Museum)

Lorenzo Costa: Head of an old Man (Berlin Print-Room)

Lorenzo Costa: Allegorical Figure of Fortune (Berlin Print-Room)

Lorenzo Costa: Study of female Figures adoring (British Museum)

Francesco Francia: The Annunciation with attendant Saints (Louvre)

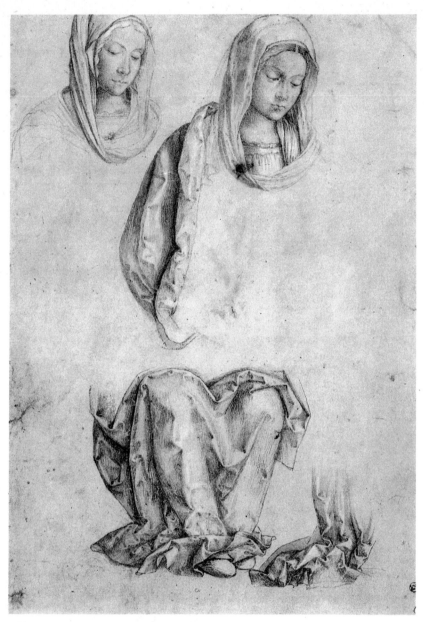

Francesco Zaganelli: Studies for a Madonna (Stockholm Museum)

Melozzo da Forlì: Head of Christ in Foreshortening
(British Museum)

Antonello da Messina: Portrait of a Youth (Albertina, Vienna)

Gentile Bellini: A Turkish Woman seated (British Museum)

Gentile Bellini: Self-Portrait (Berlin Print-Room)

Giovanni Mansueti: A Miracle of the Cross (Uffizi, Florence)

Giovanni Bellini: Study of a Man seated (Coll. Mr. A. G. B. Russell)

Follower of Giovanni Bellini: Pietà (British Museum)

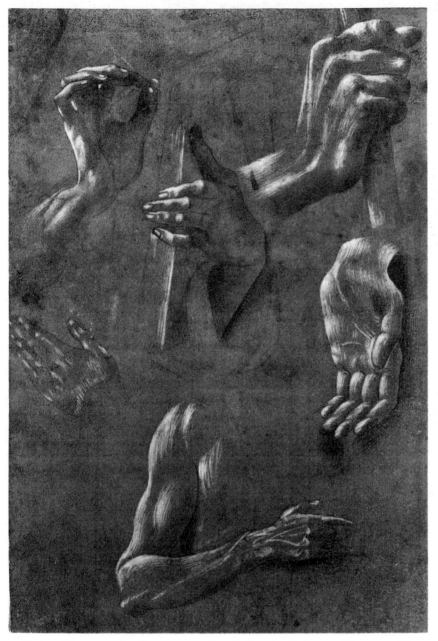

Alvise Vivarini: Studies of Hands (Coll. Mr. F. Lugt, Maartensdijk)

Cima da Conegliano: St. Jerome
(Uffizi, Florence)

Cima da Conegliano: Landscape (British Museum)

Jacopo de Barbari: Seated Woman (Cleopatra?)
(British Museum)

Style of Lazzaro Bastiani: Madonna della Misericordia
(British Museum)

Vittore Carpaccio: Studies for a Procession (Louvre)

Vittore Carpaccio: The Adoration (Uffizi, Florence)

Vittore Carpaccio: Head of an old Man (Coll. Mr. Henry Oppenheimer)

Vittore Carpaccio: Design for an Altarpiece (Dresden Print-Room)

Follower of Carpaccio: Virgin and Child (Louvre)

The Master of the Allendale Adoration: The Adoration
(Royal Library, Windsor)

Bartolomeo Montagna: The Assumption of the Virgin
(Munich Print-Room)

Bartolomeo Montagna: Christ Enthroned (?)
(Royal Library, Windsor)

Bartolomeo Montagna: Virgin and Child (Musée Wicar, Lille)

Giovanni Buonconsiglio: Christ at the Column (Louvre)

Francesco Bonsignori: Portrait of Gian Francesco Gonzaga
(Uffizi, Florence)

Francesco Morone: The Virgin enthroned with Saints
(Uffizi, Florence)

Liberale da Verona: The Presentation (British Museum)

Vincenzo Foppa: The Justice of Trajan (Berlin Print-Room)

Bernardino Zenale?: Christ shown to the People (British Museum)

Ambrogio Borgognone: The Assumption of the Virgin (Berlin Print-Room)

Ambrogio da Predis: Head of a Youth in Profile
(Bayonne Museum)

The Master of the Archinto Portrait: Study of a Hand
(Ambrosiana, Milan)

Bernardino dei Conti: Head of an old Man in Profile
(Coll. Mr. Henry Oppenheimer)

The Master of the Pala Sforzesca: Portrait of Massimiliano Sforza
(Ambrosiana, Milan)

Bramantino: Study of a kneeling Figure (Berlin Print-Room)

Andrea Solario: Portrait of a Man (British Museum)

Boltraffio: Study for a Head of the Virgin (Christ Church, Oxford)